CHRISTMAS FAVORITES

FOR VIOLIN DUET

Arranged by Michelle Hynson

ISBN 978-1-5400-2925-6

HAL•LEONARD®

Visit Hal Leonard Online at
www.halleonard.com

Contact us:
Hal Leonard
7777 West Bluemound Road
Milwaukee, WI 53213
Email: info@halleonard.com

In Europe, contact:
Hal Leonard Europe Limited
42 Wigmore Street
Marylebone, London, W1U 2RN
Email: info@halleonardeurope.com

In Australia, contact:
Hal Leonard Australia Pty. Ltd.
4 Lentara Court
Cheltenham, Victoria, 3192 Australia
Email: info@halleonard.com.au

BLUE CHRISTMAS

Violin

Words and Music by BILLY HAYES
and JAY JOHNSON

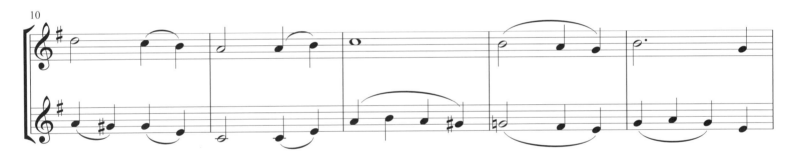

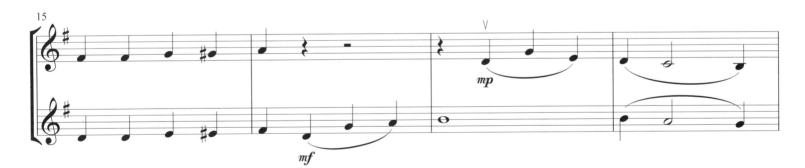

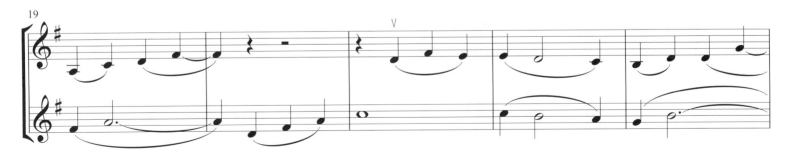

CAROLING, CAROLING

VIOLIN

Words by WIHLA HUTSON
Music by ALFRED S. BURT

With a lilt

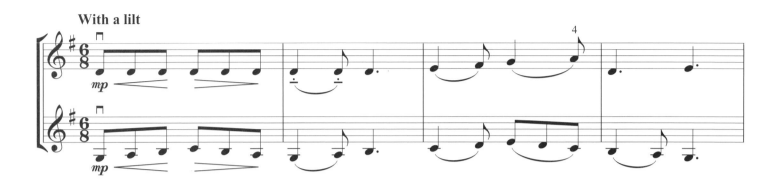

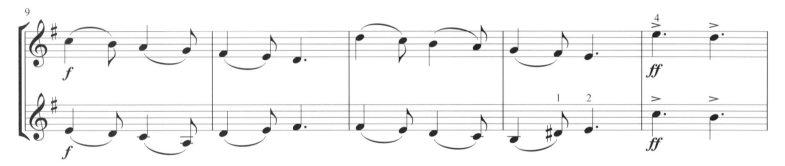

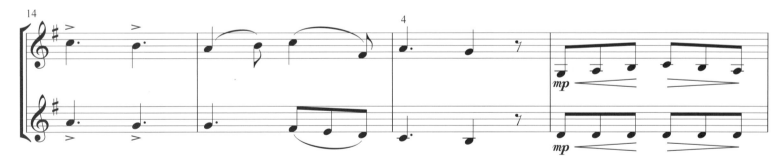

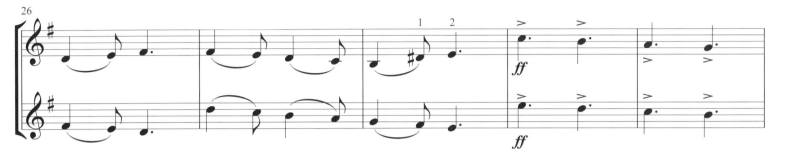

THE CHRISTMAS SONG
(Chestnuts Roasting on an Open Fire)

VIOLIN

Music and Lyric by MEL TORMÉ
and ROBERT WELLS

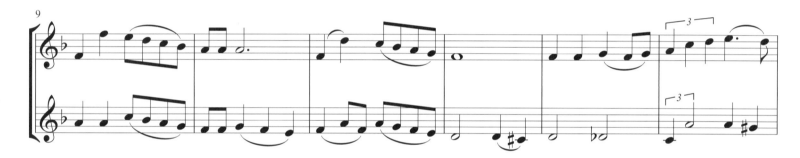

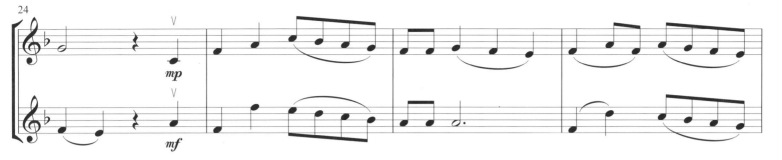

CHRISTMAS TIME IS HERE

from A CHARLIE BROWN CHRISTMAS

VIOLIN

Words by LEE MENDELSON
Music by VINCE GUARALDI

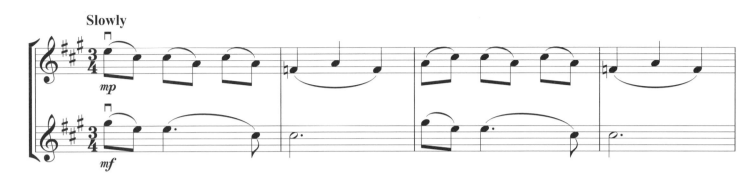

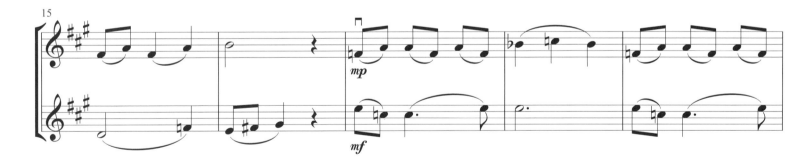

DO YOU HEAR WHAT I HEAR

VIOLIN

Words and Music by NOEL REGNEY
and GLORIA SHAYNE

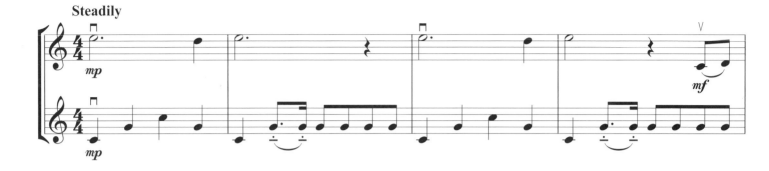

FELIZ NAVIDAD

VIOLIN

Music and Lyrics by
JOSÉ FELICIANO

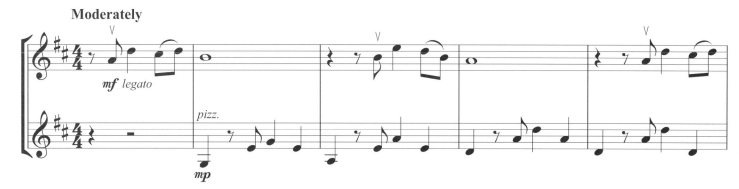

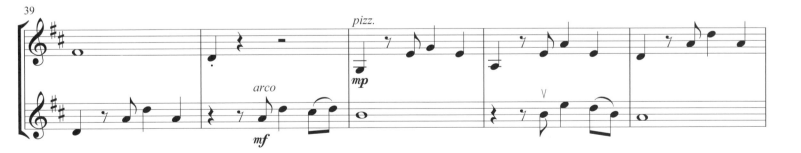

FROSTY THE SNOW MAN

Violin

Words and Music by STEVE NELSON
and JACK ROLLINS

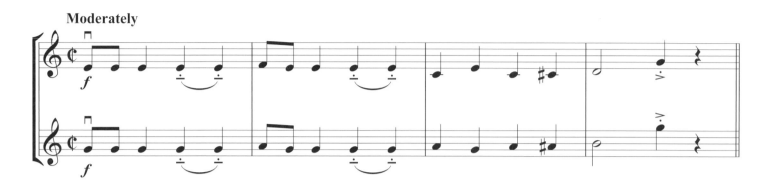

GROWN-UP CHRISTMAS LIST

VIOLIN

Words and Music by DAVID FOSTER
and LINDA THOMPSON-JENNER

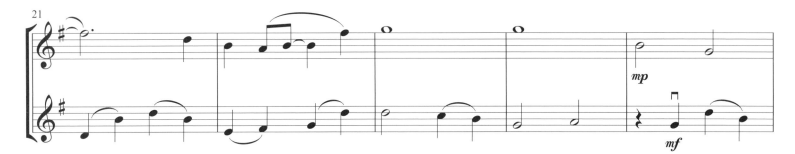

HAPPY HOLIDAY

from the Motion Picture Irving Berlin's HOLIDAY INN

VIOLIN

Words and Music by
IRVING BERLIN

HAVE YOURSELF A MERRY LITTLE CHRISTMAS

from MEET ME IN ST. LOUIS

VIOLIN

Words and Music by HUGH MARTIN
and RALPH BLANE

Moderately

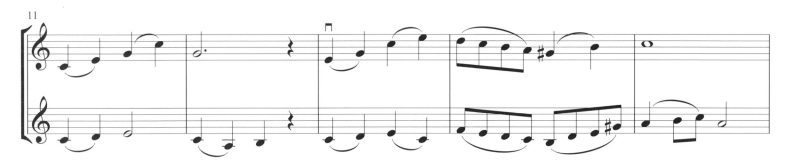

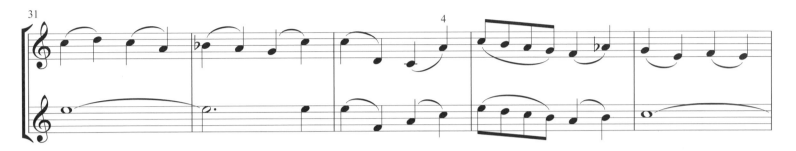

HERE COMES SANTA CLAUS
(Right Down Santa Claus Lane)

VIOLIN

Words and Music by GENE AUTRY
and OAKLEY HALDEMAN

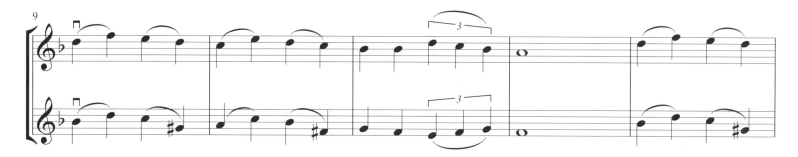

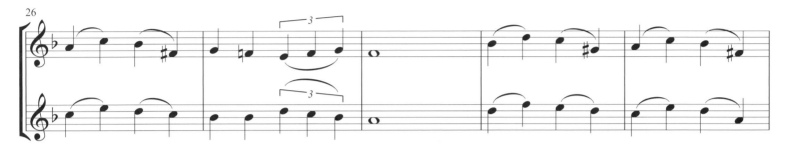

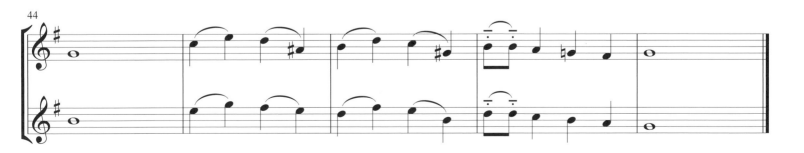

A HOLLY JOLLY CHRISTMAS

VIOLIN

Music and Lyrics by
JOHNNY MARKS

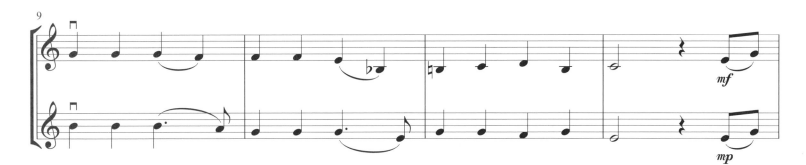

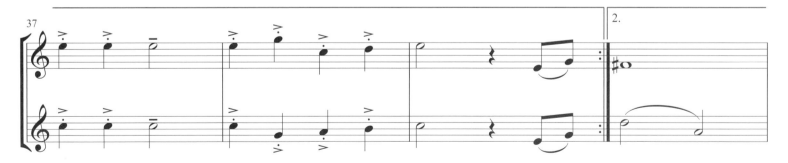

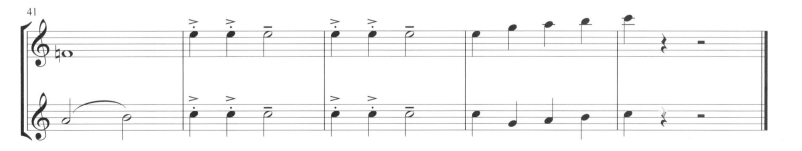

(There's No Place Like)
HOME FOR THE HOLIDAYS

VIOLIN

Words and Music by AL STILLMAN
and ROBERT ALLEN

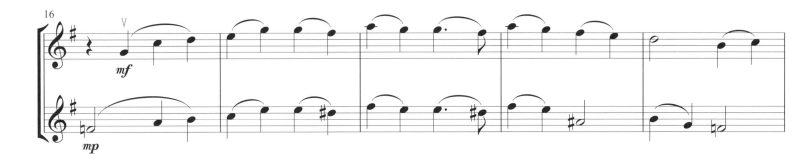

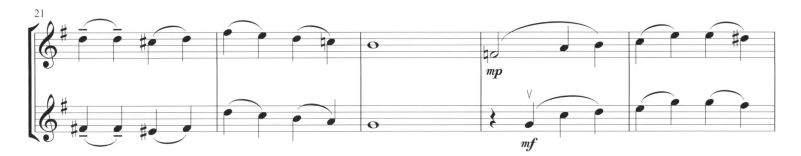

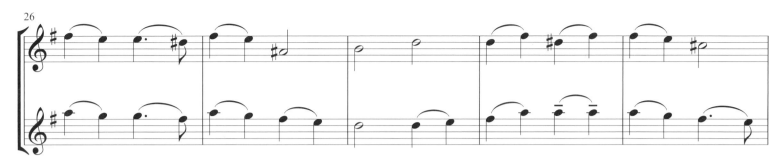

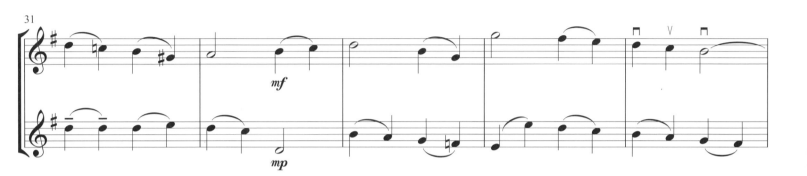

I HEARD THE BELLS ON CHRISTMAS DAY

VIOLIN

Words by HENRY WADSWORTH LONGFELLOW
Adapted by JOHNNY MARKS
Music by JOHNNY MARKS

Moderately slow

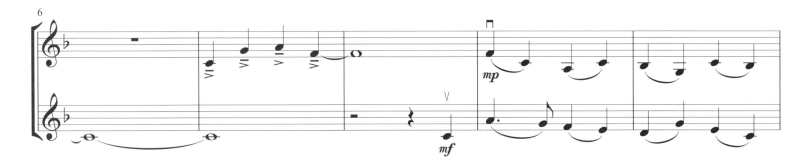

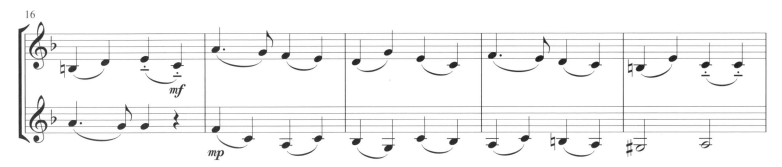

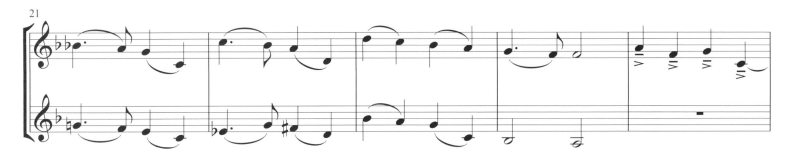

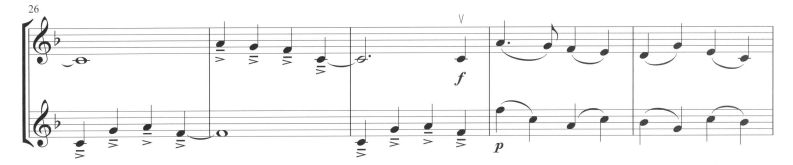

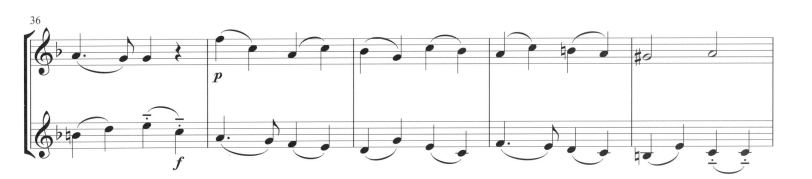

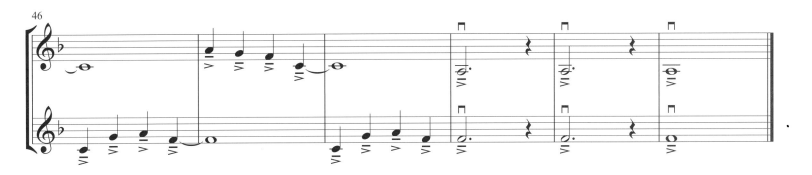

I SAW MOMMY KISSING SANTA CLAUS

VIOLIN

Words and Music by
TOMMIE CONNOR

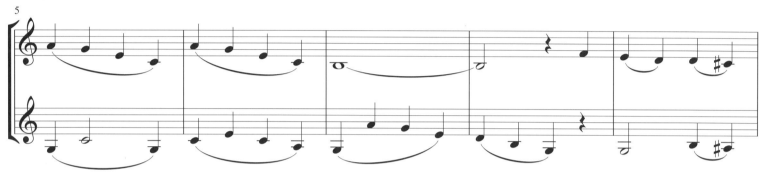

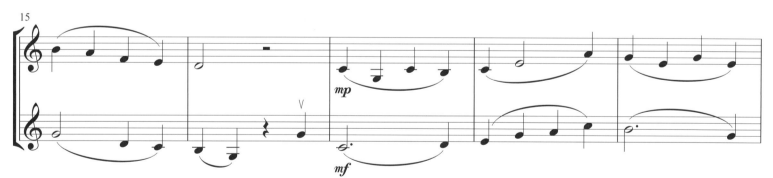

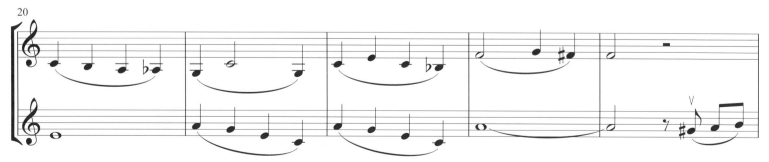

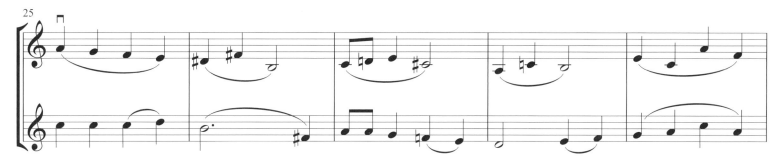

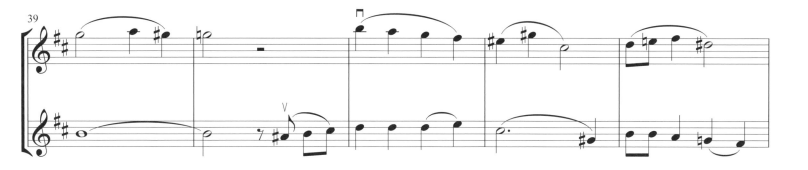

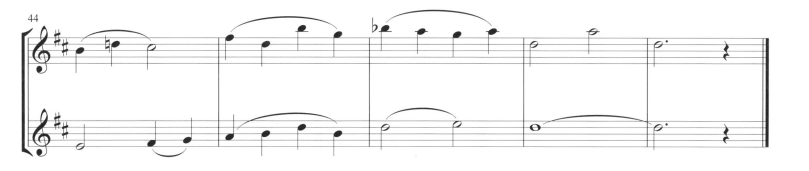

I'LL BE HOME FOR CHRISTMAS

VIOLIN

Words and Music by KIM GANNON
and WALTER KENT

Moderately slow, in 2

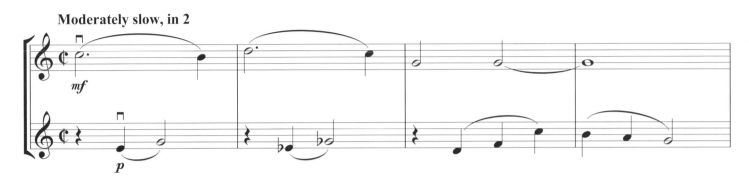

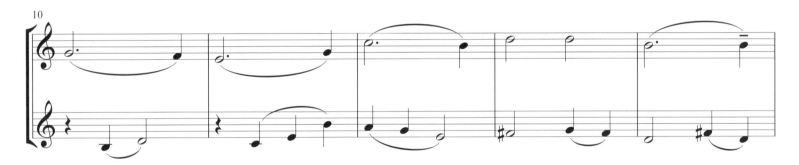

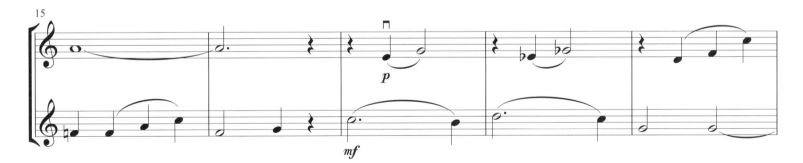

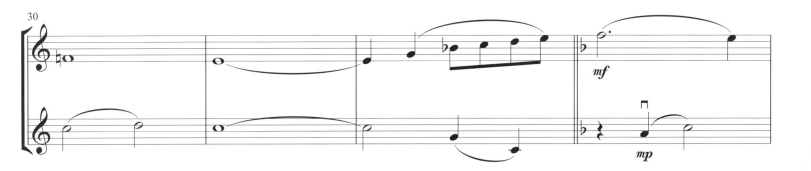

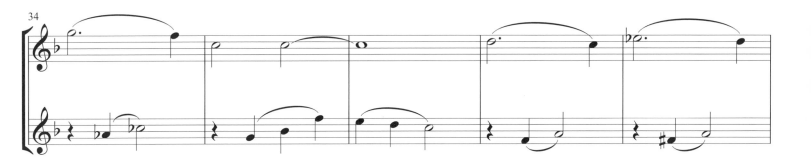

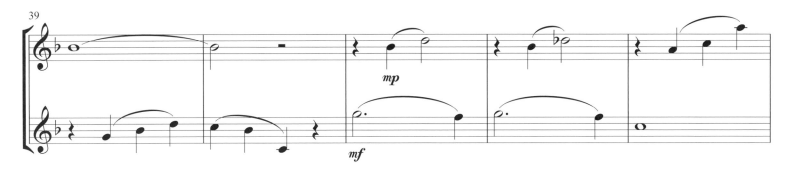

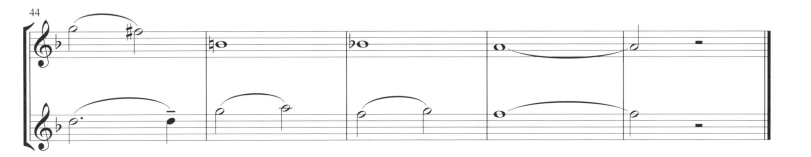

IT'S BEGINNING TO LOOK LIKE CHRISTMAS

VIOLIN

By MEREDITH WILLSON

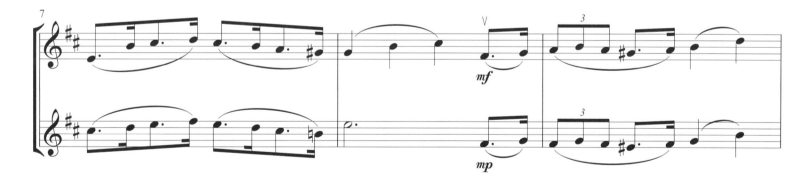

To Coda ⊕

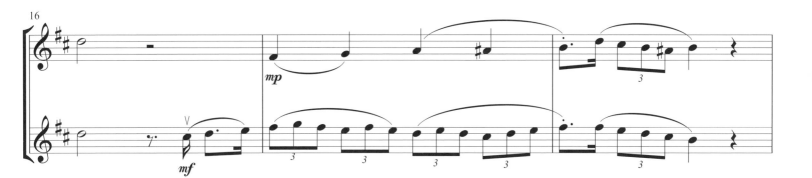

D.S. al Coda

CODA
⊕

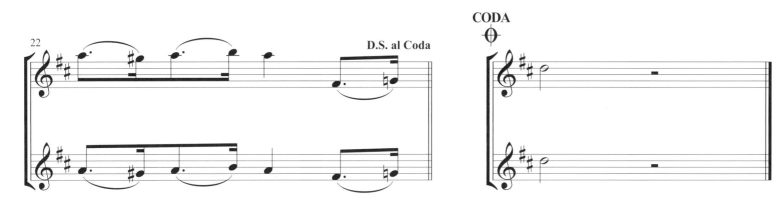

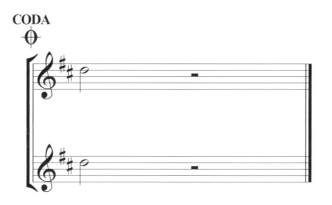

JINGLE BELL ROCK

VIOLIN

Words and Music by JOE BEAL
and JIM BOOTHE

LET IT SNOW! LET IT SNOW! LET IT SNOW!

VIOLIN

Words by SAMMY CAHN
Music by JULE STYNE

THE LITTLE DRUMMER BOY

VIOLIN

Words and Music by HARRY SIMEONE,
HENRY ONORATI and KATHERINE DAVIS

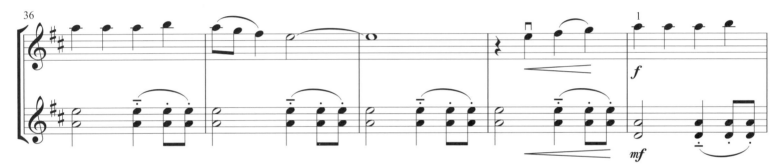

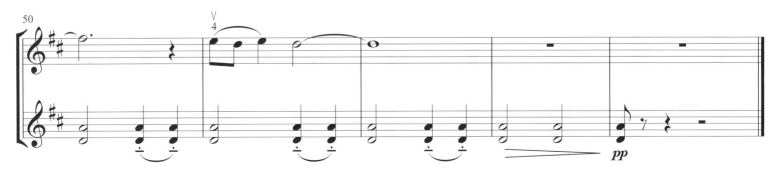

MARY, DID YOU KNOW?

VIOLIN

Words and Music by MARK LOWRY
and BUDDY GREENE

D.S. al Coda

MISTLETOE AND HOLLY

VIOLIN

Words and Music by FRANK SINATRA,
DOK STANFORD and HENRY W. SANICOLA

THE MOST WONDERFUL TIME OF THE YEAR

VIOLIN

Words and Music by EDDIE POLA
and GEORGE WYLE

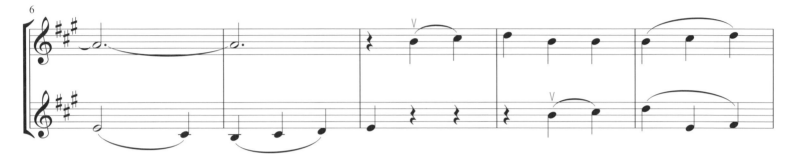

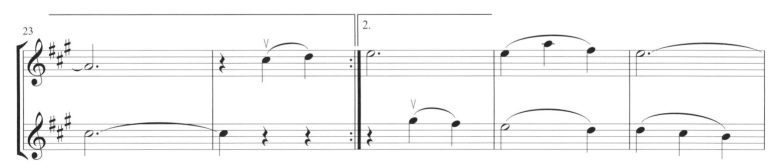

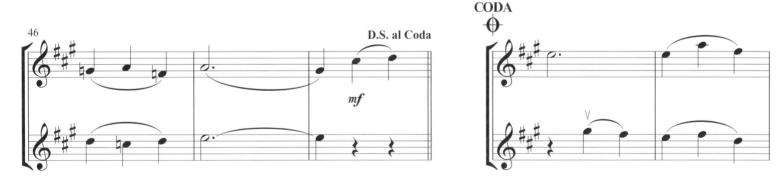

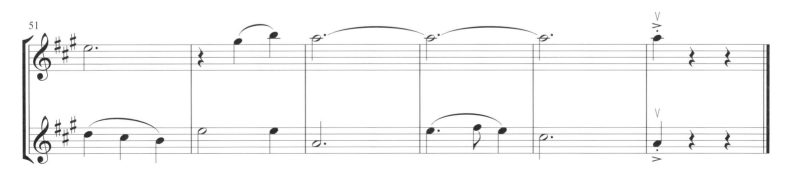

ROCKIN' AROUND THE CHRISTMAS TREE

VIOLIN

Music and Lyrics by
JOHNNY MARKS

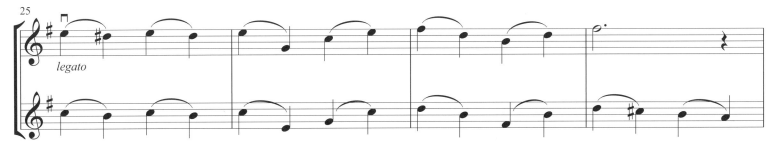

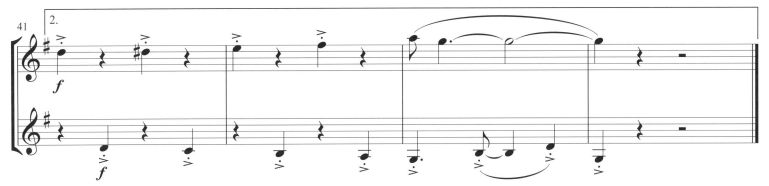

RUDOLPH THE RED-NOSED REINDEER

VIOLIN

Music and Lyrics by
JOHNNY MARKS

Moderately fast, lightly

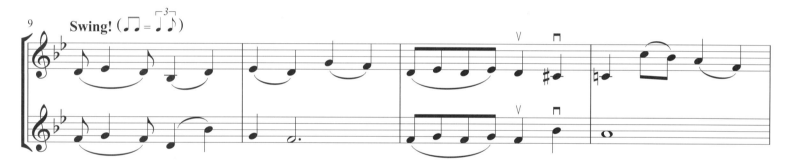

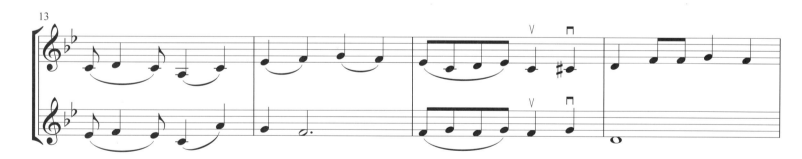

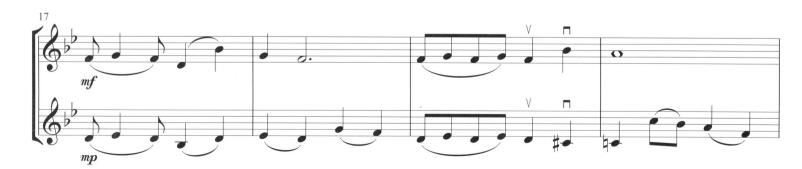

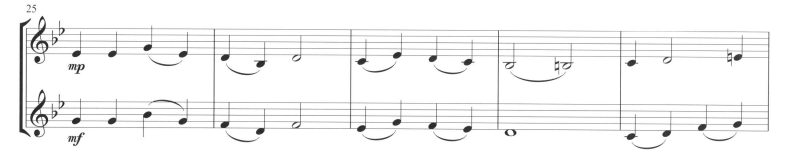

SANTA CLAUS IS COMIN' TO TOWN

VIOLIN

Words by HAVEN GILLESPIE
Music by J. FRED COOTS

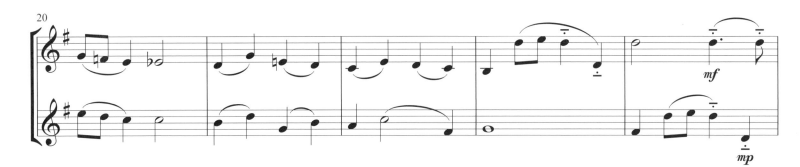

SILVER BELLS
from the Paramount Picture THE LEMON DROP KID

VIOLIN

Words and Music by JAY LIVINGSTON
and RAY EVANS

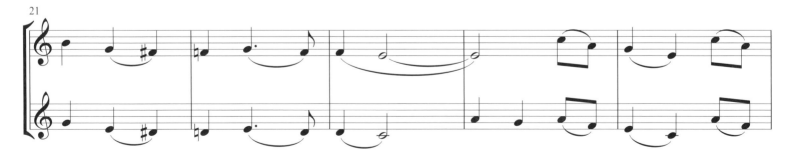

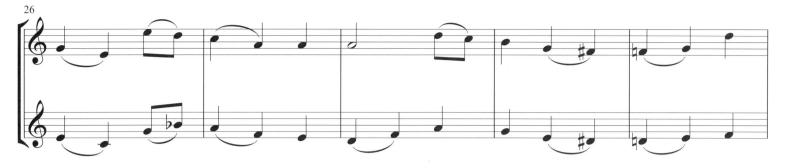

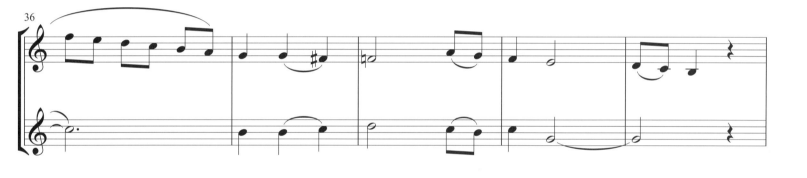

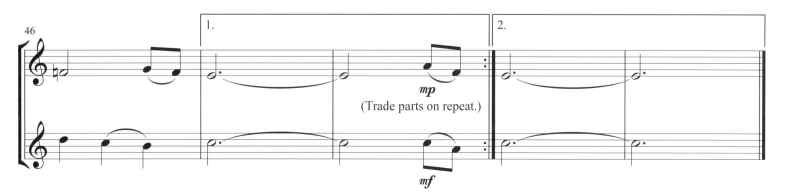

(Trade parts on repeat.)

SLEIGH RIDE

VIOLIN

Music by
LEROY ANDERSON

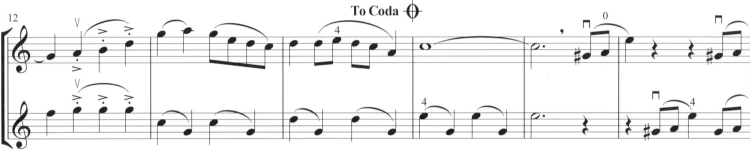

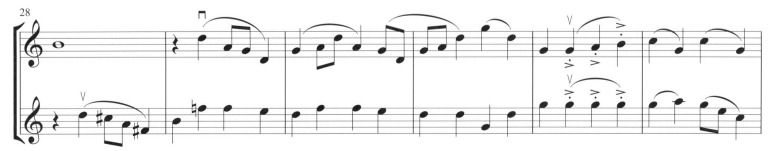

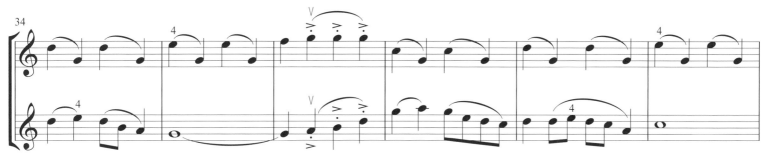

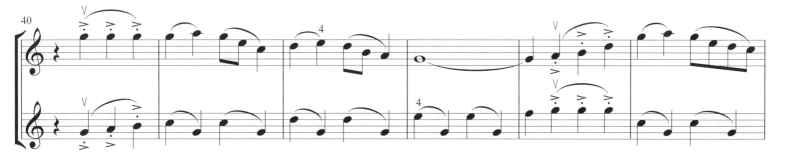

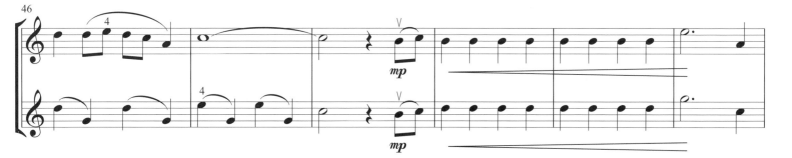

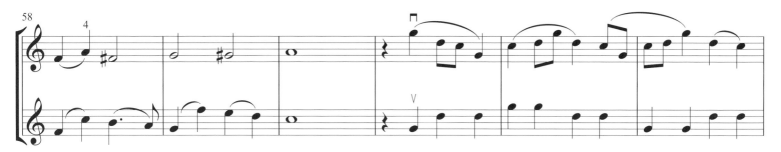

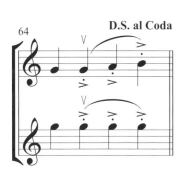

WE NEED A LITTLE CHRISTMAS

from MAME

VIOLIN

Music and Lyric by
JERRY HERMAN

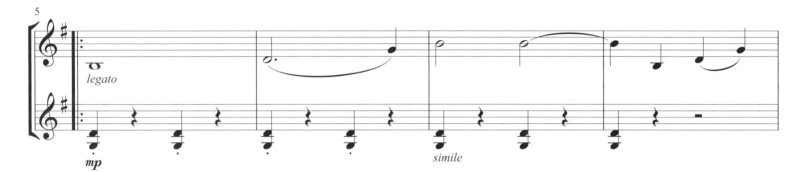

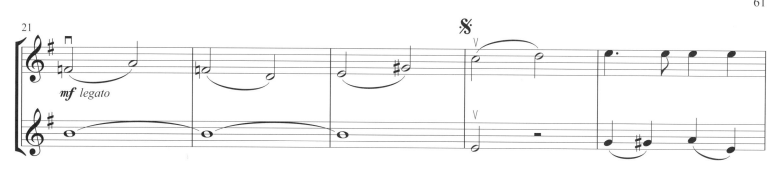

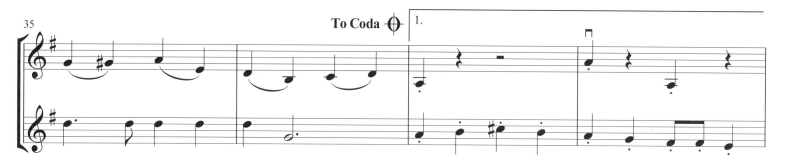

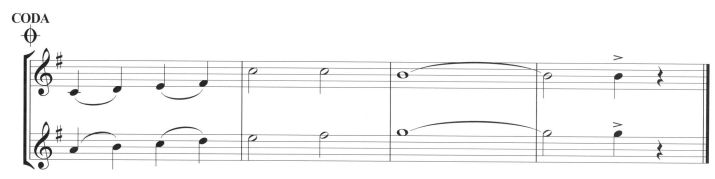

WHITE CHRISTMAS

from the Motion Picture Irving Berlin's HOLIDAY INN

VIOLIN

Words and Music by
IRVING BERLIN

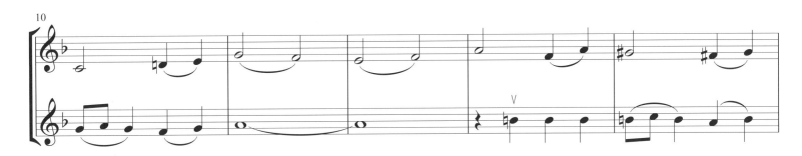

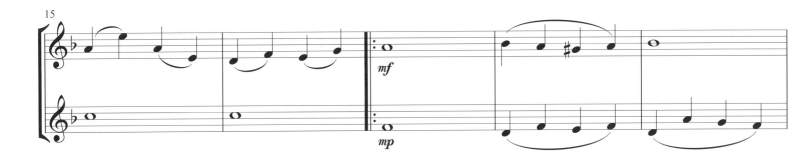

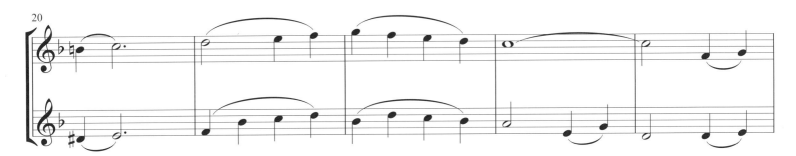

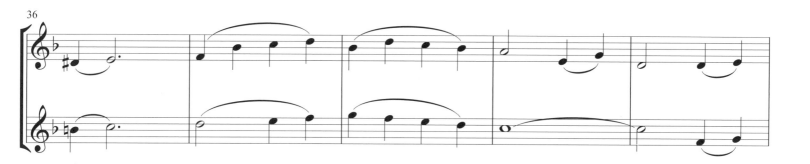

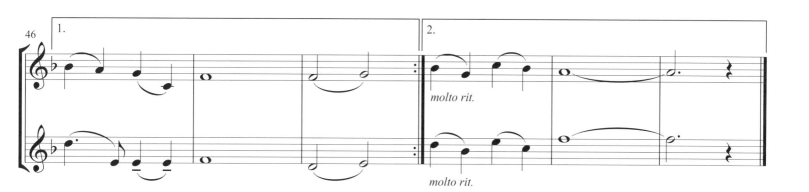

VIOLIN DUET
COLLECTIONS

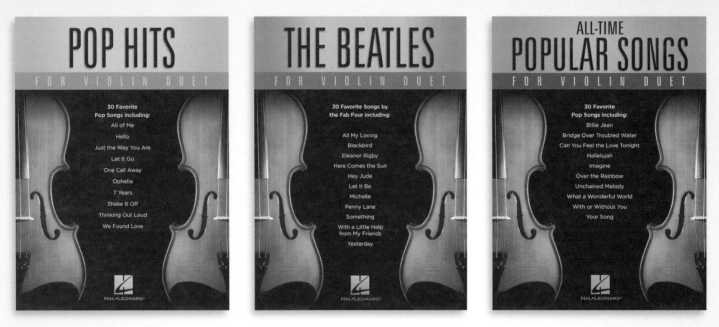

These collections are designed for violinists familiar with first position and comfortable reading basic rhythms. Each two-page arrangement includes a violin 1 and violin 2 part, with each taking a turn at playing the melody for a fun and challenging ensemble experience.

ALL-TIME POPULAR SONGS FOR VIOLIN DUET

Billie Jean • Bridge over Troubled Water • Can You Feel the Love Tonight • Hallelujah • Imagine • Over the Rainbow • Unchained Melody • What a Wonderful World • With or Without You • Your Song and more.

00222449 . . . . $14.99

THE BEATLES FOR VIOLIN DUET

All My Loving • Blackbird • Eleanor Rigby • A Hard Day's Night • Hey Jude • Let It Be • Michelle • Ob-La-Di, Ob-La-Da • Something • When I'm Sixty-Four • Yesterday and more.

00218245 . . . . $14.99

POP HITS FOR VIOLIN DUET

All of Me • Hello • Just the Way You Are • Let It Go • Love Yourself • Ophelia • Riptide • Say Something • Shake It Off • Story of My Life • Take Me to Church • Thinking Out Loud • Wake Me Up! and more.

00217577 . . . . $14.99

DISNEY SONGS FOR VIOLIN DUET

Beauty and the Beast • Can You Feel the Love Tonight • Colors of the Wind • Do You Want to Build a Snowman? • Hakuna Matata • How Far I'll Go • I'm Wishing • Let It Go • Some Day My Prince Will Come • A Spoonful of Sugar • Under the Sea • When She Loved Me • A Whole New World and more.

00217578 . . . . $14.99

www.halleonard.com

Prices, contents, and availability subject to change without notice.